Shari Lewis

PRESENTS

101 GAMES
and
SONGS
for Kids to Play and Sing

Library of Congress Cataloging-in-Publication Data: Lewis, Shari. Shari Lewis presents 101 games and songs for kids to
play and sing / by Shari Lewis. p. cm. SUMMARY: Presents seventy-four games, including outdoor games, board games,
card games, and games using paper and pencil. Includes the scores and lyrics for twenty-seven songs.
ISBN 0-679-82271-2 (trade) — ISBN 0-679-92271-7 (lib. bdg.) 1. Games—Juvenile literature.
2. Singing games—Juvenile literature. [1. Games. 2. Songs.] I. Title. II. Title: Shari Lewis presents one hundred
and one games and songs for kids to play and sing. III. Title: 101 games and songs for kids to play and sing.
IV. Title: One hundred and one things for kids to do. GV1203.L4746 1993 790.1'922—dc20 92-20572

Manufactured in the United States of America 10 9 8 7 6 5 4 3 2 1

Shari Lewis

PRESENTS

101 GAMES and SONGS

for Kids to Play and Sing

By Shari Lewis
Illustrated by Lisa Goldrick

Random House New York

◦◆◦ CONTENTS ◦◆◦

Songs

☆ ☆ *Introduction* ☆ ☆

To the kids, for whom this book is intended:

"Kids" is a word that has so many meanings. It ranges from little kids to big ones, and includes both boys and girls; it's young people who live in cities, suburbs, and on farms. Some kids have to play indoors much of the time because of cold or rainy weather, while others can spend most of the year playing in the sun, in parks and backyards, on playgrounds and beaches.

One thing that I know for sure: Kids love to play! So here's a book full of games to play indoors and out, alone or with friends, wherever you live. Some are kicky, unusual activities, while others are time-tested favorites that *you* may not have gotten around to testing. As for the songs—well, most are game songs, in which either you do actions to go with the words or the words themselves are goofy and fun to sing.

I'll bet it'll take you ages and ages to try all 101 songs and games in this book—and when you've done 'em all, you can start all over again! I'd love to know how old you are and which are your favorites… Will you write and tell me, please? Just drop me a line in care of Random House, Inc. (201 East 50th St., NY, NY 10022) and I'll send you a picture of Lamb Chop and me in return.

Shari Lewis

To any parents peeking at these pages:

I wish that I could tell you the appropriate age level for each game, but that truly isn't possible, for (as you parents know) children vary tremendously. Every game in this book is safe, and I leave it to you to decide which will work for *your* child. All the activities will interest the child who can read the book by him- or herself.

To help the environment (and save money), bring home paper or plastic cups from fast-food restaurants. Rinse 'em out. With these cups, your kids can play a lot of games (like Itty-Bitty Basketball and Paper Cup Pool). Also save those used sheets of aluminum foil. Wash 'em, and then crumple into foil balls for tossing games.

I've picked action songs that are fun for the kids, and *have* been fun for kids since *I* was a kid. This is my rule of thumb because it is the only guarantee I have that someone might know the melodies of these perennials. Of course, we've included melody lines and chord symbols for those who can read 'em. I hope that singing along with your youngsters will bring back—and generate—many happy memories.

Active Games

Most of these active games can be played with only one friend, and they're guaranteed to get both of you up on your feet and laughing. Have fun!

1 Remember!
△ ▲ △ ▲

Turn your back as a friend puts no less than ten items on a table (tiny toys, spoons and forks, coins, or anything else that will fit under a big box lid).

Then your friend covers the items with the lid, and you turn to face the table. Your buddy lifts the lid for a slow count of five, then drops the lid so you can no longer see the things beneath.

How many things can you remember in thirty seconds? How many can your friend remember? See who can name the greatest number of hidden items.

2 Fumble
● ○ ● ○ ●

You can play this game with one friend, or with lots at a party or club meeting.

The first player is blindfolded and handed six alphabet blocks (or any small toys without wheels). From a standing position, the blindfolded player drops the blocks on the floor in front of him or her. Then the player must stoop down and pick up all six blocks in thirty seconds. It's fun to watch all the fumbling.

Does this game sound too easy to be a good game? Don't knock this block game until you try it!

3 *Otedama*

◇ ◇ ◇ ◇

In Japan, children play beanbag games called Otedama. You can play this one alone or with friends.

To make five small beanbags, fill socks with dried beans and knot them (of course, you can also buy beanbags at the toy store). If you do make your own, make them little and don't stuff them too full—they should be soft and floppy.

This beanbag game is like jacks: Put four beanbags on the table or floor in front of you, then throw the fifth up in the air. Now with that same throwing hand, pick up another beanbag and shove it between any two fingers of your *other* hand. Then use your free hand to catch the beanbag that you've tossed as it's coming down. Repeat, each time ramming a beanbag between the next two fingers. When you're done, you should have four beanbags securely tucked between the fingers of one hand.

If the tossed bag hits the ground before you've tucked the other one between your fingers, you lose your turn, and the next player takes over.

The first person to tuck all four beanbags securely between the fingers is surely the winner!

4 *Ouch!*

♦ ♦ ♦ ♦

This is a game for two players. The first person's hands are held out with the palms down. The other person's hands go palm up, *below* (and lightly touching) the first person's downturned hands. The player with hands below tries to strike the tops of the other player's hands before he or she can pull them out of reach. When the "bottom" player misses, change positions.

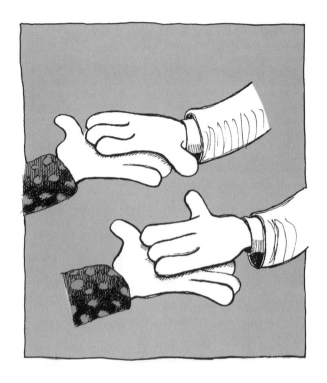

5 *Very Soft ball*

○ ○ ○ ○

This is fun to do with one friend or with teams of two, for it's as amusing to *watch* as it is to *play*.

Put down two big bowls next to each other and fill one bowl with cotton balls. One player is then blindfolded and given a spoon. The aim of the game is to scoop up as many cotton balls as possible (using just the spoon) and transfer them to the other bowl. When the first player thinks that he or she has gotten all the cotton balls transferred, then it is the next player's turn. Don't forget to count the cotton balls, though, because the player (or team) who moves the most cotton balls wins!

Everybody will move very slowly and gingerly, because cotton balls weigh so little that no one will be able to tell if they have any on their spoon or not. And no touching with the other hand is allowed!

6 Pushy Pushy

▲ ▼ ▲ ▼ ▲ ▼ ▲

It's best to play this game with someone who's close to your own size.

Two friends sit back to back on the floor and lock their arms together at the elbows. Each then tries to get up by pushing against the other.

If more than two friends have gotten together, play Pushy Pushy with teams, each made up of a pair of players. The first team that stands up wins!

7 Posture

☐ ☐ ☐ ☐ ☐

Balance a box cover on your head (a board game box cover works best) with two paper cups at your feet. You must stoop down, pick up one cup, and place it upright on the box cover balanced on your head. Then stand up straight. Next you stoop again, place the second cup on the box cover, and stand up a second time without knocking over either cup.

If you can do this, you have my admiration—especially if you can do it in less than a minute!

8 Pick Up Beans

● ● ● ● ●

Next time you're playing with a friend, play Pick Up Beans. Put some dried beans onto a table and, using a straw, pick up the beans one at a time and plop them into two nearby cups. How? Place one

open end of the straw in your mouth, the other against the smooth surface of a bean, and breathe in. Keep breathing in until you've moved the bean above the cup. To release the bean, breathe out.

When all the beans have moved to the cups, count and see who got the most!

9 *Ring Thing*

○   ○   ○   ○

Give each player a sheet of facial tissue. Tell players to start at one corner and roll their sheets of tissue into sticks. Then everyone curves around the two ends of his or her paper sticks until the ends meet and form a ring. These two ends get twisted around each other so the ring won't open. Now all are ready to play.

Here's how: The players tilt their heads back a little, and each places the paper ring on his or her forehead. The object of the game is to get the ring to slide down the face and into the mouth.

Yes, it can be done, if you shake your head just a little at a time. I have the best luck when I get the ring onto my eye, then blink my lashes to shake it down onto my cheek, and finally reach up my tongue and guide the ring into my mouth.

The first player to get that little Ring Thing between the lips is the big winner!

Ball Games

10 *Easy Does It!*

◆   ◆   ◆   ◆   ◆   ◆

Both players hold out their left hands, palm down, so that the *sides* of their hands are touching. On the back of one player's hand, place a ball. Now try to transfer the ball to the back of the other player's hand.

No fair using your other hands to help. Can you do it?

11 Clapzies

❖ ❖ ❖ ❖ ❖

A blindfolded player holds a ball. Then that player must toss the ball up into the air and clap his or her hands once before catching the ball. The other player must pick up and give back to the blindfolded player the balls that are missed. That will keep everybody busy indoors or out!

See who can catch the ball the most times in forty-five seconds.

String Games

12 Knots and Not Knots

♦ ● ♦ ● ♦

Each player gets a very long string, ribbon, or rope. At a signal, each player begins to tie knots in his or her own length of string. What the players *don't* know is this: At a second signal, the players must *untie* the knots. (As a variation, have each player untie the knots that his or her neighbor to the right has made!)

13 Wind 'n' Wind

△   △   △   △   △

For each player, tie one end of a very long string to the back of a chair placed across the room. Now tie the other end of the string to the player's pointer finger.

At the signal, all players begin to wind their strings completely around their own fingers again and again, *using that finger only*. Each player must wind the entire length of the string around his or her finger and cross the room to stand beside his or her own chair. The first player to reach the chair is, of course, the winner.

Be careful to tie the string *loosely* around the finger, and warn all players not to wind so tightly that they cut off their circulation.

Here are some goofy games for groups—they're not just for parties. Try 'em at your scout meeting or at the playground. And tell your friends I said "hello."

Group Games

14 Bedlam in the Barnyard

△ □ ○ △ □ ○

In this game, you must change your voice, or it will give you away!

Blindfolded, the player who is "it" stands in the middle of a circle of players. "It" turns and points to someone in the circle and names an animal that the chosen player must imitate by making the right sound for the creature named. If "it" guesses the name of the player making the animal sound, that player then becomes "it"; otherwise "it" must point to another player and try again.

Variation: Sing-a-Song Blindman's Buff

Blindfolded, "it" points to a player and names a song. The chosen player must sing that song in a disguised voice or with an accent so that "it" can't tell who is singing.

MEOW!

15 Magic Key

❖ ◆ ❖ ◆ ❖

In plain view, set out a big lock and a pile of numbered, varied keys, along with a pad and a pencil.

As each guest arrives, he or she chooses which key will fit the big lock. On the pad, the guest writes his or her name next to the *number* of the selected key.

When all the guests have chosen, they gather to try the keys, and the winner gets a prize!

16 Cat's Whiskers

▲ ▼ ▲ ▼ ▲ ▼ ▲ ▼ ▲

I learned this game in Japan.

Starting at any corner, roll diagonally—and tightly—a single sheet of facial tissue (the kind you use to blow your nose). Roll it to form a thin stick (this is easier if you keep wetting your pointer finger and thumb). Moisten the loose corner and press it against the roll. That's your "whisker." Now you can play Cat's Whiskers!

Hold your whisker horizontally and put it right above the middle of your upper lip. (Grip it in place by curling your upper lip toward your nose.) Remove your fingers. The object of this game is to pass the whisker from person to person (I mean, from "cat" to "cat") without using your hands.

This is a *very* friendly game!

17 Hats Off

▽ ▽ ▽ ▽

Ask everyone who is coming to the party (or meeting) to bring a hat—the weirder the better. Then gather everyone into a circle, with each person wearing a hat.

Choose someone to lead the game. When the leader calls out "one," each player puts his or her right hand on the head of the person to the right, grasping the hat that is resting on that person's

head. At the count of "two," each player takes that hat and puts it on his or her *own* head. As the game goes on, the leader speeds up or slows down the counting, and all kinds of confusion crop up!

Whoever drops a hat on the floor is out.

The leader can also shout "Reverse!" Then, instead of using the right hand to grab the hat of the player to the right, each person must now use his or her *left* hand to grab the hat of the player to the *left*, and the direction of the game is reversed. Throughout the game, the leader can continue to reverse the action. As hats are dropped, players are eliminated until only one player remains.

Of course, you can vary the game by starting with each player holding on to his or her *own* hat, then placing it upon a neighbor's head. Either way, my hat's off to the winner!

18 *Giggle Belly*
■ □ ■ □ ■

The first player lies face up on the floor. The second player lies down with his or her head resting on the stomach of the first player. The head of the third person goes on the stomach of the second player, and so on (*see picture*).

Now, you want to have a laugh? **Here's how**: The first person says "ha." The second person then says "ha-ha." Then the third person says "ha-ha-ha" and so on, with each player adding one more "ha." After the last player adds his or her "ha," return to the first player again.

The "ha's" must be said *without laughing* (which isn't easy!), and the player who manages to keep a straight face the longest is the winner. With all the tummies bouncing the heads around, not only does it *sound* funny, but it *feels* funny too!

Races

These races can be played with as few or as many of your friends as you want. (You can play some of the games by yourself, by racing against the clock.) For bigger groups, it is a good idea to choose a person to be a judge (grownups are sometimes good for this). The judge starts off a race by calling out "Ready, Set, Go!," watches to make sure the players are doing the races correctly, and judges who the winner is at the end.

Some races seem easier than they actually are. These are all toughies, but you won't believe me until you try 'em!

19 *Sour Sweep*

♦ ● ♦ ● ♦

Give each person a broom and a lemon. Holding the broom with the straws facing up, each player uses the broom handle to push the lemon across a bare floor to a goal line. The broom handle must not be lifted off the floor, nor can the lemon be hit or shoved. It should be pushed and rolled all the way.

This game is a real challenge (and real fun) because lemons invariably want to roll in any direction *except* straight ahead!

20 *Big Foot Shuffle*

□ ● □ □ ● □

Don't throw away those empty shoe boxes—save 'em for the Big Foot Shuffle.

If there are only two players, each steps into two open shoe boxes (one on each foot) and races across the room without taking either foot out of the boxes. Just shuffle those boxes along the floor, and the first player to reach the opposite side of the room is the winner!

Or play the Big Foot Shuffle as a team relay race! When the first player makes it across the room and steps out of the boxes, the next team member steps in.

Each team has its own pair of shoe boxes, and the teams run the race at the same time.

21 *Kneezies*

◇ ◆ ◇ ◆ ◇

Here's one you can do all by yourself, but it's also fun to watch a whole bunch of people at it.

Put a ball between your knees and walk all the way across the room and back again. Twenty seconds is all you've got, so move it!

22 Back Up! Click, Click!

△ △ ○ △ △

For some reason, kids under seven or so can't seem to do this trick. See which of your friends can do it the fastest.

Line up with your backs to the "finish line"—which could be the wall across the room or the fence across the playground. Then, putting one foot exactly in front of the other, toe to heel, each person walks backward as fast as he or she can.

When each player has reached the finish line, he or she does the second part of this race: the player stands with heels a foot apart, bends his or her knees, and jumps forward. While in the air, the heels are clicked together *twice,* and the player lands with feet apart. The first to click heels twice is the big winner!

23 Hop 'n' Stop

● ○ ● ○ ● ○ ●

To set up the game, put one small toy down at your feet, then take two steps away from it. There, place a second toy on the floor. Take two more steps and place a third toy on the floor. Finally, take two steps past the third toy, turn around, and start the fun!

Raising one foot off the floor, hop to each toy and pick it up until you have retrieved all three toys. But don't let your other foot touch the floor even once. Consider yourself a winner if you can do this in forty-five seconds.

24 Lucky Duck! Hopzies!

■ ■ ■ ■ ■

Mark two lines about eight feet apart—one is the starting line, the other the turning line. At the starting line, players sit on their heels, grabbing their ankles in the squat position. At the command "Go!," they start to race by waddling like ducks until they reach the turning line. Then the players turn around and head back to the starting line—and don't let go of those ankles!

Next, each player bends one leg behind him or her and grasps that ankle. Then he or she hops from starting line to turning line and back to starting. The first one there is the winner.

Tossing Games

25 *Um-balla*

▲ ▲ ▲ ▲

Tossing games can be a disaster indoors, but not if you're tossing rolled-up socks!

Open an umbrella (no, I'm *not* superstitious) and put it on the floor. Players stand about ten feet away from the umbrella and take turns tossing sock balls into it. You score one point each time your sock ball stays in the umbrella. The first player to earn twenty-five points is the winner.

as close to the first as possible. The aim of the game is to get the second glove to touch the first.

26 *Handshake*

△ ▲ △ ▲ △

Fill two gloves with clean torn stockings or tissue paper. Close up the openings of the gloves with rubber bands.

The first player throws one glove, then the second player pitches the other glove

27 Egg Carton Cup-It

◇ ◇ ◇ ◇ ◇

Use a crayon to write a different number from 1 to 12 in each little "cup" in the bottom of a cardboard egg carton. Place the prepared egg carton on the floor four or five feet from the players.

Give each player six of a different object to toss. For example, one gets six buttons, the other six beans, the third pennies. The contestants then pitch their small objects into the egg carton. When an object lands (and stays) in a cup, the player who tossed it receives the number of points written on the bottom of that cup.

The first player to earn fifty points wins.

Outdoor Games

Down near the water, where the sand is wet—that's where you can draw game boards on the beach with a stick, a key, or your finger, and play lots of your favorite games.

28 Pitch-a-Word

○ ○ ○ ○ ○

In the wet sand or on a flat piece of ground, draw a really big circle. All around the circle, write the letters of the alphabet. Each player then stands in the center of the circle and pitches a small stone, trying to hit letter after letter in order to spell out a three-letter word. Each word can only be used once, and whoever gets the most words wins!

For a challenge, try this game spelling longer words.

29 Tic-tac-Checkers

Here's a new twist on an old game— and you can play it in the packed sand.

Draw a tic-tac-toe pattern in the hard sand. But instead of drawing X's for one player and O's for the other, use shells of two different shapes. (Or one player can use shells while the other uses pebbles or pennies.)

The new twist? If your tic-tac-toe game is about to end in a tie (as so often happens), try this before that last box is filled: continue playing almost as if the game were checkers. You don't jump *over* the other person's "man" (as in checkers); rather, you get to move into the other player's box and take away his or her man. Beware! Your pal can do the same to you, and the last man left on the sandy board is the winner.

Before you start, both players have to decide whether, when you get to the "almost checkers" part of the game, you can move only from side to side and up and down, or whether you can also move diagonally.

Of course, you can also play Tic-tac-Checkers indoors, drawing your patterns with pencil or crayon and substituting buttons and beans for shells and pebbles.

30 *Pebble Toss-It*

◆ ● ◆ ● ◆

Put a pebble on the back of your hand. Toss it in the air and catch it in your palm. Then try to do it with two pebbles, three pebbles, and even more. The player who catches the most with no spills is the winner!

31 *Gamparan*

◆ ◆ ◆ ◆ ◆

This Indonesian foot game can be played by several players, or you can enjoy it all by yourself.

Find smooth stones that are the right size to curl your toes around. When each player has a stone, draw a starting line in the dirt. One by one, use your toes to "toss" the stones as far as possible. The player whose stone flies the farthest is the winner!

32 *Yote*

□ □ □ □

This West African game for two players is played on a "board" scooped out in the dirt or sand. Stones, pebbles, shells—these are usually the playing pieces.

Scoop out a playing board with five indentations across, six down (*see picture*). The two players get twelve "pieces" each. For example, one gets twelve shells, the other twelve pebbles.

Each starts by putting one of his pieces into any hole. Only one object is allowed in a space at a time, and only one piece may be moved by a player as the player takes his or her turn. All of the player's pieces do *not* have to be laid down before the markers on the board can be moved. Pieces can be moved one space in a straight line either forward, backward, or sideways, but moving diagonally is a no-no.

As in checkers, the object of the game is to "capture" all of your opponent's pieces. A capture is made when a player jumps over the opponent's piece with one of his or her own pieces and removes it from the board. A player can only jump one piece in a turn. The jumper is then allowed to remove one more of the opponent's pieces from anywhere on the board.

To play indoors, staple two and a half egg cartons together, as shown, to make the board.

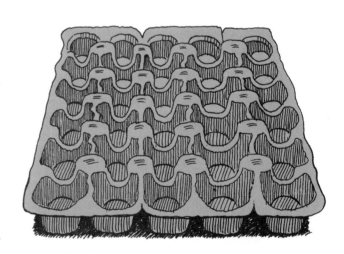

Games with Ice Cubes

Every house has ice cubes, and there's fun to be had with them—but play these games in the bathroom or kitchen, or a meltdown is likely to make a mess. Of course, these games are fun to play outdoors as well.

33 *Fork It Over*

❖ ❖ ❖ ❖ ❖

Fill one cup to the top with ice cubes. Using only a fork, scoop out all of the cubes by sticking the fork into the cup, getting as many as you can on each forkful. Carefully drop the ice cubes into another cup. If you spill, you must load 'em all back into the first cup and start again.

Beginners, try this with a teaspoon. It's easier—but not much!

Can you transfer the cubes from one cup to the other in twenty seconds? Thirty? Can you do it *at all?*

This game can also be played with teams of two or more, or as a relay race.

34 *Dump It*

△ △ △ △

Your friend sits at your feet, facing
away from you and holds an empty cup
on his or her head. You hold a cup filled
with six ice cubes on top of *your* head.
Your challenge is to pour them into your
partner's cup as quickly as you can. Then
switch places. Can you do it without
dropping a single cube?

You might try Dump It as a relay race
at your next party or scout meeting.

35 *Dropzies*

● ○ ● ○ ● ○ ●

Place a cup on the floor right in front
of you. Now pick up an ice cube and,
holding it at chin level, drop it into the
cup. Can you drop six cubes in a row
into the cup without knocking it over?
Can you do it in forty seconds or less?

Newspaper Games

36 *I've Got a Word*
■ ■ ■ ■ ■

Cut letters from a newspaper and drop them into a paper bag. You and a friend take turns pulling out letters. Whoever is the first to make a three-letter word with the letters he or she has pulled is the winner of that round.

37 *Comic Mix-up*
▲ ■ ● ▲ ■ ●

Cut apart the frames of a comic strip and mix them up. The winner of the game is the player who can put them back together in the right order the quickest.

To make the game even harder, cut apart the frames of a couple of comic strips and mix them up. Then the challenge is to separate the comic strips from each other *and* to figure out the correct order of each set of pictures. Now see who's the fastest.

Board Games

38 *Gone Fishin'*

▲ ▼ ▲ ▼ ▲ ▼ ▲

Two people can play this game. The big circle is the pond; numbered circles all around the pond are the schools of fish (*see picture*).

Each player takes a turn, starting at any numbered circle, pointing to that circle, and counting "one" (regardless of what number is written in that circle).

Then the player continues to point and count the circles *counterclockwise*.

A player "catches fish" when he or she comes to a numbered circle that happens to match the number he or she is counting out. For example, if you started at the numbered circle 13 and counted "one," you'd be counting "three" as you pointed to the numbered circle 3. Then you would catch those three fish. A turn ends when a player has caught fish or when he or she has gone all the way around the circle (in which case, no fish are caught).

Keep track of what circles players begin on. Players must start from a different circle each time, so that each circle is used as a starting point *only once* in each game.

Keep score. After ten turns each, the player who has caught the most fish is the winner!

39 *Eight into Sixteen*

♦ ● ♦ ● ♦

Here are sixteen squares. Can you fit eight coins—four pennies and four nickels—into eight of the sixteen squares so that no two coins of the same kind are in the same line vertically, horizontally, or diagonally?

Try it—there are a couple of ways to do it! *(See one solution on page 29.)*

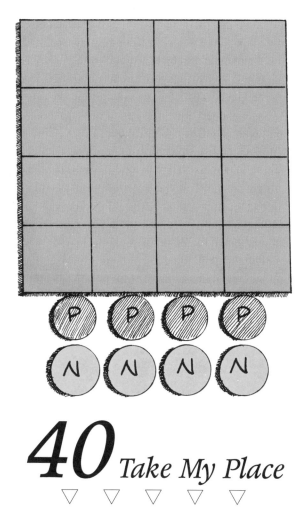

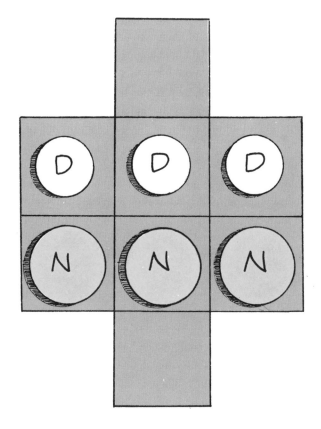

40 *Take My Place*

▽   ▽   ▽   ▽   ▽

Arrange three dimes and three nickels on the game board *(see picture)*. The aim of the game is to get the nickels where the dimes are and the dimes where the nickels are.

Here are the rules: You must take turns moving a dime, then a nickel, and so on. You may move backward, forward, sideways, or diagonally. But you can move only one square at a time, and the square that you move into must be empty.

After you've done this several times, you may want to try it *without* moving diagonally. It will be harder!

41 *To the Top!*

▲ ▲ ● ▲ ▲

You will need a nickel, a penny, and a single die (that's just one in a pair of dice) or a numbered spinner.

Two or more players can climb the mountain right on this page. Each chooses a different coin and takes a turn throwing the die (or twirling the spinner) until someone reaches the mountaintop and wins! Each move depends on the number rolled or spun.

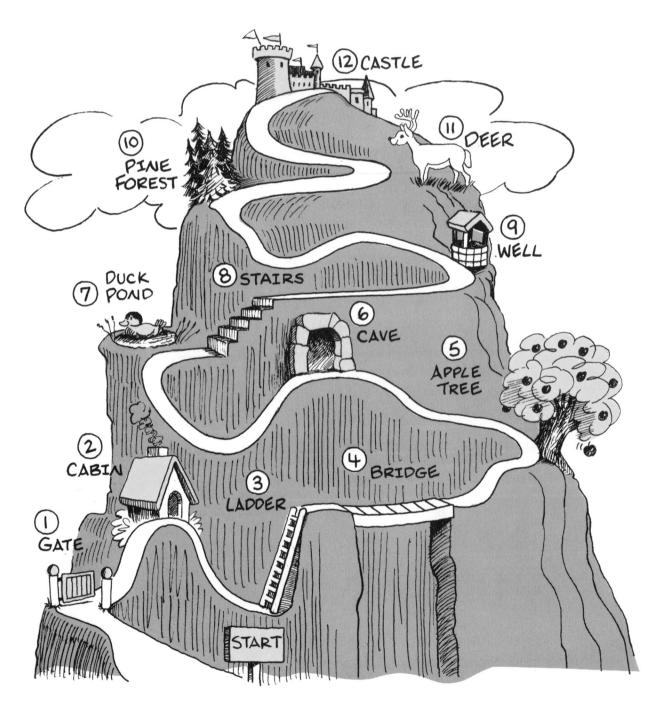

Games with Paper Cups

Solution to game #39

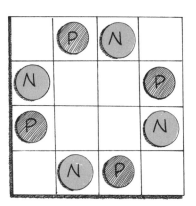

42 *Paper-Cup Pool*

▽   ▽   ▽   ▽   ▽

Tape a paper cup to each corner of a table, and one more at the midpoint of each side. The cups should hang off the edge. In the center of the table, place several buttons, balls of paper, or large beans. The point of the game is to flick the objects, one at a time, into the cups.

If two or more friends are playing, each player should have a different object to flick. The players take turns flicking, and when a player gets one of his or her objects into the cup, that person gets another turn.

43 Itty-Bitty Basketball

● ● ● ●

Tape a bottomless paper cup to a wall just above your reach. (If you happen to be sick, tired, or both—you can tape it to the foot of your bed!)

The perfect "ball" for Itty-Bitty Basket-ball can be made by crumpling pieces of aluminum foil until they are the size and shape of large marbles—round but not too firmly packed.

Shoot at your basket from a few feet away. If you're shooting baskets in bed, make lots and lots of tiny silver basket-balls—but be sure to pick them up when you're done.

44 *Cup-els*

□ ● □ □ ● □

This is a game for four or more people. Divide into teams of two players each. The pairs stand at a "starting line" and wedge a cup between their foreheads. At a signal, the teams race to a spot eight or ten feet away. There, the "cup-el" carefully bends down, picks up a toy (or small item) that has been placed on the floor at that spot, and hurries back to the starting point. The first team to reach the starting line wins!

31

45 *Wobbly Roll*

♦ ● ♦ ● ♦

You and a friend sit on the floor facing each other, about six or seven feet apart. Roll two lemons or two paper cups one at a time toward your friend. When your friend has both lemons or cups, he or she rolls them back to you. How fast can you do it? It's harder than it sounds.

You can play Wobbly Roll as a team game, too.

46 *Blow Man Blow*

○ ○ ○ ○ ○

Tear a sheet of newspaper into lots of pieces, each about one inch square. Each player puts about a dozen little pieces into his or her own paper cup. At a signal, the players try to blow the bits of paper out of their cups. Whoever blows them all out first is the winner.

As for the loser . . . why, that's the one who has to clean up!

47 *Grab-It!*

◆ ◆ ◆ ◆

Drop three foil balls into a paper cup. Toss all three balls into the air, then try to catch 'em with your hands before they drop to the floor. (You'll probably have to drop the cup in order to do this!)

Play Grab-It! with a friend or two, and see who is the first to catch all three balls.

Coin Games

48 *Fox and Geese*

❖ ❖ ❖ ❖ ❖

Use your checkerboard to play Fox and Geese. The "fox" is a quarter placed at one end of the board. The "geese" are eight pennies lined up across the opposite end of the board.

The aim of the fox is to get across the board to the opposite end. The geese want to block the fox until it can't make another move. The fox can move backward or forward, but the geese can go only straight forward. Neither the fox nor the geese can move diagonally. There is no jumping or taking away of "men." This is a blocking game.

49 *Plink!*
▲ ▲ ● ▲ ▲

Two players sit across a table from each other and take turns flicking dimes toward the opposite side of the table. The object of the game is to get your dime nearest to the edge without letting it fall *plink!* onto the floor. Flick the dimes with a snap of your pointer finger.

Each player had better start with a handful of coins, since they tend to go *plink!* a lot, and picking 'em up isn't as much fun as playing one coin after another.

50 *Wiggle*
◇ ◆ ◇ ◆ ◇

Here's a game that everyone can play together, but it's best if one of your friends just stands by and watches, to make sure you all play it *right*.

Here's how: You and your friends lie flat on your backs on the floor. Each player balances a dime on his or her nose so that it's perfectly level. Now you all wiggle your *noses only* and try to be the first to wiggle that dime off. Seem awfully easy? Moving only your nose, you'll be lucky if you can do it at all, no less do it *first*.

As you play Wiggle remember to keep your mouth *shut!* (You want the dime on your nose, not in your mouth.)

The "watcher" has to make sure that all players are wiggling only their noses, not shaking their heads.

51 Tabletop Hockey

● ● ● ●

Three coins are the "pucks," and the playing field is a small table. To create a "net," one player (the "goalie") extends pointer finger and pinkie over the edge of the table, keeping the rest of the fingers tucked away (*see picture*).

The other player is the "shooter," who tries to snap three coins toward the goal from wherever they land when they are dropped on the table. The goalie drops the pucks—hoping that they'll land in the worst possible spots on the table.

The shooter continues to shoot until one of the pucks goes over the edge of the table. Then the goalie becomes the shooter. The new goalie drops the coins, and the new shooter snaps them toward the net.

The winner is the player who snaps the most pucks into the net.

52 *Nim*

◇ ◇ ◇ ◇

People who are game nuts call this challenge Nim, but no one seems to know why!

Set up three rows of coins—a row with three coins, another with four coins, and one with five coins.

The aim of the game is to force the *other* person to pick up the last coin. Players can take all coins in a row or any coin within a row, but can't remove coins from more than one row at a time.

There is a secret to winning this game: On each turn, either leave *one coin in each row* or leave *an equal number of coins in two rows*. Then remove the *entire third row*.

Just be Nim-ble and follow these instructions, and you can't lose!

Card Games

53 *Horse Race*

▲ ▼ ▲ ▼ ▲ ▼ ▲

Two or four people can play, each using a different coin as his or her "horse."

Remove the four aces from a full deck of fifty-two playing cards and put them face up next to one another on a table. Next, deal out the remaining forty-eight cards face down, twelve in front of each ace (*see picture*). This is the racecourse to be run by the horses.

Each of the four players chooses an ace and the column of cards below as his or her racetrack. (If only two people are playing, each has *two* horses on the track, and each chooses *two* aces).

Each player's horse is placed on his or her ace—that's the starting position. The first player turns face up one card in his or her column, starting with the card that is farthest from the ace, and moves according to the rules below. The next player does the same, and so on. The game goes on in this way until someone wins by crossing the "finish line" (the card at the bottom of the column).

Here are the game rules:

1. If the card turned up is the same color as the ace at the head of the column, the horse advances four "lengths." (In other words, the coin moves down four cards.)

2. If the card turned up is the opposite color from its ace, the horse loses two lengths. (The coin moves up two cards.)

3. If the card turned up is a queen of *any* color, the horse loses three lengths. (Move the coin up three cards.)

4. If the card turned up is a king or jack of any color, the horse moves forward three lengths. (Move the coin down three cards.)

5. Of course, the horse can't go back any farther than the starting line (the ace).

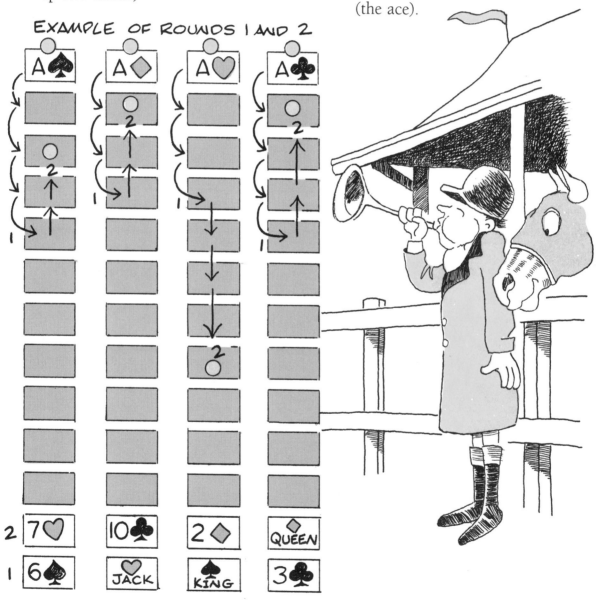

EXAMPLE OF ROUNDS 1 AND 2

54 *Murder (or Wink)*

◆ ◆ ◆ ◆ ◆ ◆

Before you start, count out as many cards from a deck as there are players. Make sure that the ace of spades is one of the cards.

The players sit in a circle so that they can see each other. One player deals the cards face down, one to each person. Each player sneaks a peek at his or her own card and then puts it back down without letting anyone else see it.

Whoever has the ace of spades is the murderer. The murderer "kills" the other players by winking at them. The players must look around the circle at each other; if the murderer winks at you, you're "dead." The victim must wait three seconds after being winked at, then die as dramatically as possible.

How do you stop the murderer? If a player thinks he or she sees the murderer wink at someone else, he or she can "accuse" the suspected murderer by saying, "I accuse (the person's name)." The accused player then turns over his or her card, and if it *is* the ace of spades, the murderer is "caught" and the game starts all over. If the card is *not* the ace, both the suspect and the accuser are out of the game.

The game continues until the murderer is caught or everyone is dead.

55 Monaco

○ ○ ○ ○

This card game is played by four people or *groups* of four people, with an additional "leader." You'll need a deck of fifty-two cards for each group of four players, plus a deck for the leader.

Have the leader shuffle one deck of cards thoroughly and then deal thirteen cards to each of the four people in each group. After shuffling his or her own deck, the leader picks one card at random and calls out its name. The player in each group of four who is holding that card removes it from his or her hand and puts it face up on the table. This goes on until any player's hand has been totally discarded. Then that person (or persons) yells "Monaco," and you have a winner!

Sometimes the game can be varied: For example, the leader might say, "Discard all threes" or "Discard all face cards," and then those "wild cards" are taken out of the hand.

56 Cover Up

□ ● □ □ ● □

Place a coin or button on the floor in front of you. The idea is to drop playing cards so that they completely *cover* the object on the floor. No fair stooping over as you drop your card!

See who can cover the item on the floor by dropping the fewest cards. Can any player do it with both eyes shut?

Paper and Pencil Games

57 *Bumper Cars*

■ □ ■ □ ■

This is a peacetime version of the board game Battleship. Each player draws a square. Inside the square, each draws four vertical lines and four horizontal lines, making twenty-five boxes in all. Across the left side of the big square, number the boxes going down 1–5. Across the top, letter the boxes A–E.

Each player hides his square from the other player and fills in any four spaces that are next to each other (up, down, sideways, or diagonal). The player fills in the four adjacent boxes by writing the name of his or her favorite car. Each car name must take up four spaces, so some will need to be abbreviated (FORD, OLDS, CHEV, VOLK, LINC, DODG, TOYO, SUBA, etc.).

Here's an example of how two players' squares might look:

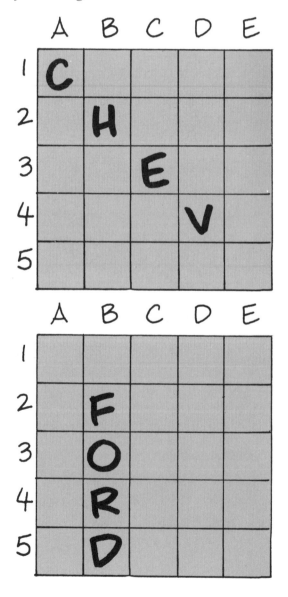

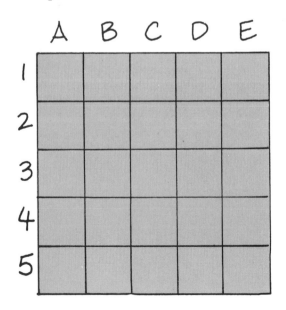

Each player takes a turn calling off a space, without being able to see where he or she is "bumping" into the other player's square. Let's say Player 1 in the game pictured above calls "D-4." Player 2 would then go *down* from D and *over* from 4. He or she would cross out the letter in that box. The Chevy would have gotten a dent near the back fender. Player 1 would mark a circle of D-4 on his or her *own* board and would not call that space again.

In order to win, you must bump into all four spaces of the other person's car. When you score a bump, the other player must tell you, so you can try to figure out where to bump next time. But since you don't know in which direction the car is parked (across, up and down, or diagonal), you can't really know whether to bump above, below, or to the left or right of the first hit. It takes a lot of bumping around to "total" your friend's car before your own gets bumped off!

58 Fifteen Every Which Way

▲ ▼ ▲ ▼ ▲ ▼ ▲

Make a square. Inside the square draw two horizontal lines and two vertical lines (like tic-tac-toe), to form a box containing nine squares. Write the number 5 in the center box.

The aim of this game is to try and insert numbers in each box so that no matter which direction you add up (horizontal, vertical, or diagonal), the numbers total fifteen.

Solution to Fifteen Every Which Way page 45.

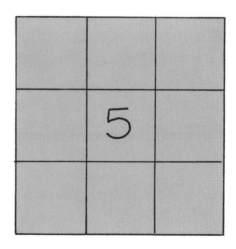

59 TV Bingo

▲ ■ ● ▲ ■ ●

Since TV is often the place to which people turn when there's nothing to do, you might as well make a game out of it!

Bingo cards usually have twenty-five squares (with a free square in the middle). Use a pencil to write, one per square, some words that you will *listen for* during a particular TV show. For example, you might pencil in *please, help!, environment, mailman, barrio.*

Or you might prefer to pencil in things to *watch for* during the show (motorcycle, covered wagon, elephant, condor, street gang, symphony orchestra, broken window, sailboat, etc.).

Place a penny on each square containing a word that is heard or an item spotted. The winning card can have five squares in a row in any direction or you can end the game when a player has *every* square filled. It's your game—you make the rules!

BINGO!

60 Word Squares

I love to play Word Squares!

Here's how: You and a friend each draw a big box. Then draw three evenly spaced vertical and horizontal lines inside. You've now divided your box into four squares across and four squares down—sixteen squares in all. Right? Let's play!

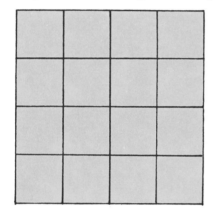

You take turns calling out letters; let's say you choose *S*. You and your friend would each write *S* in any square within your own box. (Don't let your friend see where you've written your letter.) Now, let's pretend your friend chooses *K*. You'd each write *K* in a square. The object is to try to make four-letter words, reading across or down.

Since I know a lot of four-letter words *starting* with *S*, I might put my *S* in a box along the side or on top. If my friend picks *K*, I might think of the words *sink*, *sunk*, *sick*, and *seek* and write a *K* in the box along the last row or at the bottom

(leaving empty boxes between, to be filled in with other letters).

Each player tries to put the called letter in a likely spot. When all boxes are filled, add up the points.

You earn a point for each letter of the four-letter word, and also points for words *within* words. For example, *S-I-N-K* gives you four points, and hidden inside *sink* is *S-I-N* (three points), *I-N-K* (three), and *I-N* (two). In the same way, inside *S-W-A-N* (four points) is *A-N* (two).

P	O	K	E
I	M	E	T
N	F	Y	O
K	A	S	C

POKE	4
KEY	3
KEYS	4
ME	2
I'M	2
OK	2
PIN	3
PINK	4
INK	3
IN	2
MET	3
AS	2
TO	2
TOTAL 36	

S	P	Y	O
I	O	A	F
N	E	C	K
K	M	E	T

SINK	4
SIN	3
INK	3
IN	2
SPY	3
ME	2
POEM	4
NECK	4
MET	3
ACE	3
OF	2
TOTAL 33	

61 *Pick a Number*

❖   ❖   ❖   ❖   ❖

On little slips of paper, write the numbers 1–25. Fold each little piece of paper in half, then drop them all into a large box or bag.

You and a friend take turns picking out numbers, one after another. Place the slips of paper you've chosen in front of you. When all the little papers have been pulled, each of you can add up your own total. Highest score wins.

62 Super Tic-tac-toe

✖ ● ✖ ● ✖

Tic-tac-toe is a dumb game. It works on a formula, and anyone who knows the formula can beat anyone who doesn't. And *everyone* knows the formula. Super Tic-tac-toe is much more fun.

Instead of the usual grid (two lines down, two across), draw a four-line grid:

Now play in the same way as tic-tac-toe—but score the game like this (high score wins):

One point for three in a row (in any straight line—horizontal, vertical, or diagonal)

Two points for four in a row

Three points for five in a row

You can even play the game on a bigger grid; try six lines (seven spaces) per row, and make up your own scoring system. Super Tic-tac-toe can be played anytime, anywhere, including at the beach on the wet sand.

▼ ▲ ▼ ▲ ▼ ▲ ▼

9	1	8
7	5	3
2	9	4

ate = 8   1 = 1   stick = 6
free = 3   5 = 5   7 = 7
For = 4   9 = 9   to = 2

it—"For 9 to free 5, 7 ate 1 stick."

Here's how you can remember

Solution to Fifteen Every Which Way.

63 Dot, Dot, Dot

● ● ● ● ●

This is the three-sided version of the familiar make-a-square game (in which you try to complete more squares than any other player). The object of Dot, Dot, Dot is to make more *triangles* than anyone else.

Each player in turn draws a straight line from one dot to another dot. When you draw a line that is the third side of a triangle, you get to put your initial within the triangle. Having completed a triangle, you *must* then draw another line.

Here's how this three-sided game might look in progress. (As you can see, players are trying to avoid making the second line of a triangle to keep another player from completing the triangle by making the third line.)

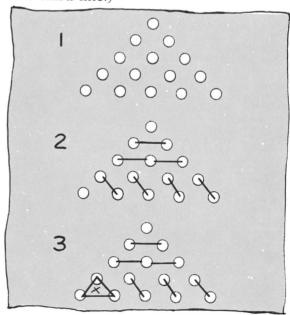

45

Mind Games

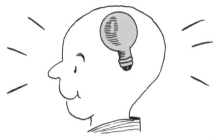

Brain twisters, brain teasers, mind bogglers, mind benders—call 'em what you will, these puzzling stories are tricky, so think twice before you answer!

64 Movie Theater Surprise

❖ ❖ ❖ ❖ ❖

Miss Michaels left the movie theater and walked toward the unlighted parking lot where she had left her car. There were no artificial lights or moonlight, yet she was able to spot her car from a block away. How could she see it?

Solution: She'd been to an afternoon show, and it was broad daylight!

65 Clean and Dirty

● ○ ● ○ ● ○ ●

Two miners came out of a coal shaft. One came out dirty; the other was clean. The clean miner went over to a pump and washed himself. Strangely enough, the dirty miner went home without washing. Why?

Solution: The dirty miner looked at the clean miner, assumed that *he* was clean too, and didn't think it was necessary for him to wash. But the clean miner was horrified by the dirty face of the other, so he went to scrub up.

46

66 Slow Boat

△ ▲ △ ▲ △

A man wanted to buy the slowest boat made in the country, so he put an advertisement in the local newspaper. Three captains answered his ad. To decide which boat was the slowest, he told the three captains to race across the lake and back. The three set out, but by the end of the day none had returned. Each was trying to prove that his boat was the slowest.

How should this man have arranged the race to find out which boat was really the slowest?

Solution: The man should have asked each captain to pilot the boat of one of the *other* captains. Then each captain would have been sure to go as fast as possible in the other boat to prove that his own boat was the slowest.

67 Double Trouble

□ □ ● □ □ ● □ □

Two boys fill out registration forms for summer camp. The director sees that they have the same parents, live at the same address, and have the same date of birth. The only difference is that one is named Tony and the other is Adam. When asked "Are you twins?," they both say no. If their answers are true, and they have the same mother and father, how can they *not* be twins?

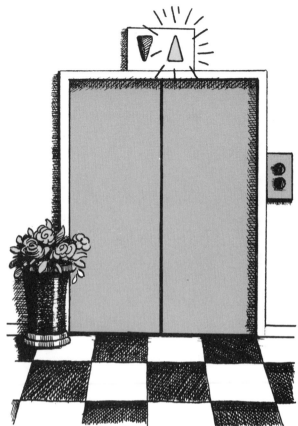

Solution: Tony and Adam are two of a set of triplets!

68 What's Up?

◆ ◆ ◆ ◆ ◆

A man gets into the elevator in his apartment building and pushes the button. He goes to the main floor, gets out, and goes to work. At the end of the day, when he comes home, he gets into the same elevator, pushes a button, goes to the fifth floor, and walks up two more stories. Why?

Solution: The man is a midget. He can reach the low button for the main floor, but he lives on the seventh and can't reach up to the button for his own floor.

Car Games

I've never gotten used to going for a "nice long drive." I just can't seem to sit still! Even before any kids ask, I'm the one who whines, "Are we almost there yet?" If you get bored in the car too, here are some games that will help make that "nice long drive" seem a little shorter.

69 Map Tap

Two players sit in the backseat of a car (or on the living room floor) and open a road map across their laps. One player silently picks out the name of a place on the map and says, "I see a town" (or a river, or a mountain range) "beginning with *S*" (or whatever letter the place name starts with) "and ending with *O*" (or whatever letter the place name ends with). The other player then has two minutes to locate it. He or she taps over the map with a pointer finger while the first player says "hot" or "cold," as the tapping finger gets closer to or farther from the chosen spot.

After two minutes, the second player gets a chance to choose a secret location. Whoever can locate the most places in under two minutes is the winner.

70 *Geografun*

○　○　○　○　○

This game can be played in a car, train, or plane . . . or sitting around a campfire or kitchen table!

First you name a place, *any* place: village, town, city, national park, country, continent, waterfall, river, ocean, mountain range—anything that can be found on any map, anywhere. After you name your place, your friend must name a place that begins with the *last letter* of the place name that you said. Then you (or a third player) must think of a place name that begins with the last letter of the *previous* place named, and on and on.

For example, if I said "Los Angeles," you might say "San Francisco," because Los Angeles ends with *S* and San Francisco begins with *S*. Then you (or the third person) might call out "Ohio," because San Francisco ends with *O*—the first letter in Ohio. The next player would have to name another place beginning with the letter *O*.

71 One Mile

◇ ◇ ◇ ◇ ◇

Here's a game that you can't play at home, unless you live in a trailer! It's a great car game, for when you are on the go!

Someone in the front seat is picked to watch the odometer (the gauge that ticks off the miles traveled). Everyone else (except the driver!) closes his or her eyes, and no one talks for what they think is one mile. When each person thinks a mile has gone by, that person yells out "One mile!" The person in the front seat says nothing, and all other eyes stay shut until the odometer watcher sees that *exactly* one mile has passed. Then the odometer watcher calls out "One mile!" The player who had guessed closest is the winner, and the game starts again.

72 Game with a Name

Going far in a car? Play a game with a name!

Lots of cities and towns have names with the same ending—such as *-dale* (Scarsdale, Hillsdale, Scottsdale) and *-polis* (Annapolis, Minneapolis, Indianapolis). When you get into the car, spread a big road map across a lap or two. Pick an ending, then race to see who can find the most places that end with those letters.

Even if you aren't going anywhere at all, you can play Game with a Name in bed, on the floor, or on a table!

73 Do This and Do That

The first player does something—makes a motion, says something, sings a bit of a song, makes an animal noise. Then that player points to a second player, who repeats what the first did and adds something of his or her own. The third player repeats what both the first and second players did, then adds to it . . . and so it goes.

The game might go like this: The first player screams "Help!" The second player screams "Help!," then sings a short phrase of "Yankee Doodle." The third player screams "Help!," sings the short song phrase, and sticks out his tongue.

Any player who makes a mistake or forgets the sequence is out of the game. The winner is the one left after everyone else is out.

74 Stinky Pinky

◆ ● ◆ ● ◆

Two words that rhyme—that's how you start. When you've thought of a rhyming pair of one-syllable words, make up a definition to describe the two-word phrase—but don't give it away! Here are some sample Stinky Pinkies.

◇ A bulb to use when it's dark (night light)

□ A piece of music with words, that goes on and on and on (long song)

◇ A gruesome tale (gory story)

□ A high, solid fence (tall wall)

◇ Excellent logs (good wood)

□ A tidy chair (neat seat)

◇ Rain that falls on pretty plants (flower shower)

□ A sunburned fellow (tan man)

◇ What you get when you compress garbage (trash mash)

□ A stupid finger (dumb thumb)

◇ A race that you really enjoy (fun run)

Take turns being the player who makes up the rhymes and the one who guesses.

75 The Ants Go Marching

❖ ❖ ❖ ❖ ❖

In this song you have to find a rhyme for each number—but the fun is to make each of these rhymes as goofy as possible.

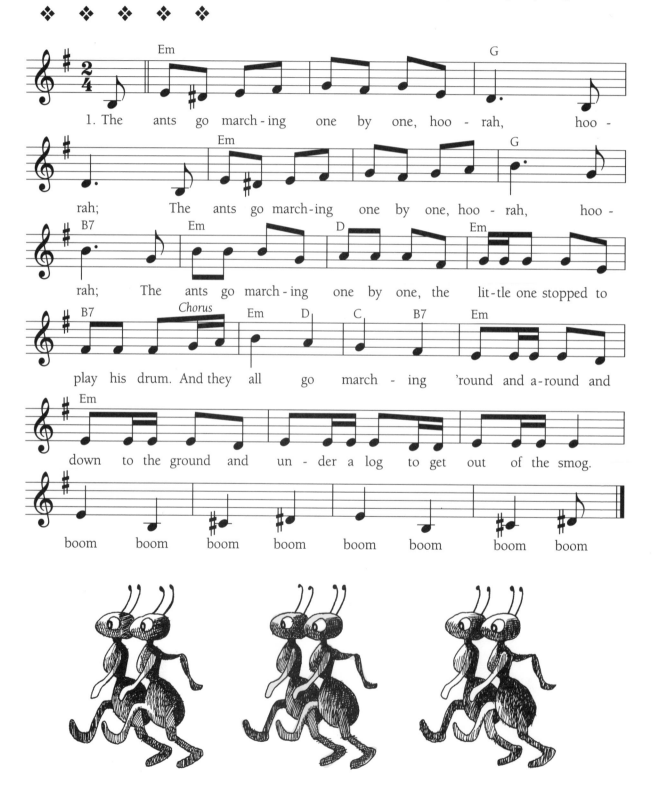

Em   G

1. The ants go march-ing one by one, hoo-rah, hoo-

Em   G

rah; The ants go march-ing one by one, hoo-rah, hoo-

B7   Em   D   Em

rah; The ants go march-ing one by one, the lit-tle one stopped to

B7   *Chorus*   Em   D   C   B7   Em

play his drum. And they all go march-ing 'round and a-round and

Em

down to the ground and un-der a log to get out of the smog.

boom boom boom boom boom boom boom boom

2. The ants go marching two by two, hoorah, hoorah;
   The ants go marching two by two, hoorah, hoorah;
   The ants go marching two by two, the little one stepped
   in a blob of glue (or "sneezed and said ah-choo!").
   Chorus

3. The ants go marching three by three, hoorah, hoorah;
   The ants go marching three by three, hoorah, hoorah;
   The ants go marching three by three, they laughed
   "ho ho, ha ha, hee hee."
   Chorus

4. And so on!

76 The Bear Went Over the Mountain

This is a *very* old song, with a new ending that will "pay off" the screams and howls that run all the way through.

1. The bear went o-ver the moun-tain, The bear went o-ver the moun-tain,
2. He saw an-oth-er moun-tain, He saw an-oth-er moun-tain,

The bear went o-ver the moun-tain, To see what he could see.
He saw an-oth-er moun-tain, So what do you think he did?

Chorus 1: So what do you think he saw? *(howling scream)*
Chorus 2: So what do you think he did? *(louder scream)*

So what do you think he saw? *(howling scream)*
So what do you think he did? *(louder scream)*

3. He climbed the other mountain,
   He climbed the other mountain,
   He climbed the other mountain,
   To see what he could see.

   Chorus 1

4. He saw another mountain,
   He saw another mountain,
   He saw another mountain,
   So what do you think he did?

   Chorus 2

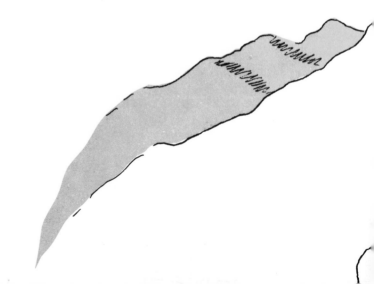

56

5. He climbed the other mountain,
   He climbed the other mountain,
   He climbed the other mountain,
   To see what he could see.
   Chorus 1

6. He saw another mountain,
   He saw another mountain,
   He saw another mountain,
   So what do you think he did?
   Chorus 2

   Spoken: "He kept on climbing, to this very
   day—and" (very fast, pointing behind
   everyone) "look out, there he is now!"
   (bloodcurdling yell)

77 B-I-N-G-O

◇   ◇   ◇   ◇   ◇

This is a song game. Each time you repeat the spelling part, you leave out another letter. Instead, you clap for that beat. By the end of the song, you will be clapping for each letter.

1. There was a farm-er had a dog, and Bin-go was his name-o. B - I - N-G-O, B - I - N - G - O, B - I - N - G - O, and Bin-go was his name - o.

2. . . . (Clap)-I-N-G-O . . .

3. . . . (Clap)-(clap)-N-G-O . . .

4. . . . (Clap)-(clap)-(clap)-G-O . . .

5. . . . (Clap)-(clap)-(clap)-(clap)-O . . .

6. . . . (Clap)-(clap)-(clap)-(clap)-(clap) . . .

If you are accompanyng yourself on the guitar, you can play this song in the key of E, using the chords E, A, and B7.

78 Cabin in the Wood

This is one of those musical games in which you sing the song through once, then leave out one more word each time you repeat the song. But *don't* leave out the actions! When you're done, you'll have a song with no words, no tune, but a lot of loony actions. As you get closer and closer to the end, speed up the pace!

In a cab-in in the wood, lit-tle man by the win-dow stood.

Saw a rab-bit hop-ping by, fright-ened as can be.

"Help me, help me," the rab-bit said, "or that hun-ter will shoot me dead."

"Come, lit-tle rab-bit, come in-side, and I'll find you a place to hide."

79 Do Your Ears Hang Low?

1. Do your ears hang low? Do they wob-ble to and fro? Can you
   ears hang low, And they wob-ble to and fro. I can

tie them in a knot? Can you tie them in a bow? Can you
tie them in a knot, I can tie them in a bow. I can

throw them o-ver your shoul-der, Like a Con-ti-nen-tal sol-dier?
throw them o-ver my shoul-der, Like a Con-ti-nen-tal sol-dier.

Do your ears hang low? 2. Yes, my ears hang high.
Yes my ears hang low.

3. Do your ears hang high?
   Do they stand up in the sky?
   Do they drop down when they're wet?
   Do they stand up when they're dry?
   Do you wave them to your neighbor,
   With a minimum of labor?
   Do your ears hang high?

4. Yes, my ears hang high,
   And they stand up in the sky.
   And they drop down when they're wet,
   And they stand up when they're dry.
   And I wave them to my neighbor,
   With a minimum of labor.
   Yes, my ears hang high.

On Verses 1 and 2, yank down on your earlobes three times, on the words "ears," "hang," and "low." Now wiggle them back and forth. Then make believe you're tying an imaginary knot and an unseen bow. Next throw over your shoulder. End it the way you started, by pulling your ears three times on the same three words.

On Verses 3 and 4, yank your lobes *up* as you sing the first two lines. Now pull the lobes down, and as you sing "do they stand up," tug ears up, holding them from the top. Finally, hold one ear and shake it as you sing about waving them to your neighbor. The last line is the same as the first.

There is one spoken bar after each of Verses 1, 2, and 3:

1. And the answer to that is . . .
2. Now I have another question . . .
3. And there's an answer to that . . .

80 *Dos y Dos*

Here's a popular Spanish counting song.

In Spanish:

dos is 2
cuatro is 4
seis is 6
ocho is 8
diez is 10
diez y seis is 16
veinte is 20
veinte y cuatro is 24
treinta is 30
treinta y dos is 32

So here are
the words to this song in English:

Two and two are four.
Four and two are six.
Six and two are eight.
Plus eight, sixteen. (that is, 8 + 8 = 16)
Plus eight, twenty-four. (16 + 8 = 24)
Plus eight, thirty-two. (24 + 8 = 32)
Carlos goes to school
And I go too. (Actually the translation is "And also, *I* go.")

Dos y dos son cua-tro. Cua-tro y dos son seis.

Seis y dos son o-cho. Y o-cho, diez y seis. Y

o-cho, vein-te y cua-tro. Y o-cho, trein-ta y dos.

Car-los va al es-cue-la y tam-bién, voy yo.

81 Down by the Bay

▲ ■ ● ▲ ■ ●

Add your own actions and verses to this silly song with lots of echoes!

Down by the bay (down by the bay) where the wa-ter me-lons

grow (where the wa-ter-me-lons grow) back to my home (back to my

home) I dare not go. (I dare not go.) For if I

do (For if I do) my moth-er will say (my moth-er will

say)
1. Did you ev-er see a dog kiss-ing a hog?
2. Did you ev-er see a cat with a pol-ka dot hat?
3. Did you ev-er see a pig in a gold-en wig?
4. Did you ev-er have a time when you couldn't make a rhyme?

Down by the bay. Down by the

82 *Fish and Chips*

■ □ ■ □ ■

You need three people or three groups, because these are really three songs that go together! The harmony is great! Each person or group sings one of the songs. After a while, when you've done it a few times, you can start listening to the others, to make sure all your voices blend.

The first person (or group) sings the "One bottle pop" part through. When they begin to sing it again, the second person (or group) joins in, singing "Fish and chips." And when that's done, the third pipes in with "Don't throw your junk."

1st Song   F

One bot - tle pop, two bot - tle pop,

2nd Song

Fish and chips and vin - e - gar,

3rd Song

Don't throw your junk in my back - yard.

1st Song C7   F

three bot - tle pop, four bot - tle pop, five bot - tle pop,

2nd Song

vin - e - gar, vin - e - gar, Fish and chips and

3rd Song

my back - yard, my back - yard, Don't throw your junk in

83 Going to Kentucky

××●×●×

This is definitely a group song game. Sing it at a party or at the playground.

These are actions that go with 1–4:

1. Everyone forms a circle, with one player in the center. The "señorita" in the middle struts around, acting like a girl all decked out with roses in her hair, while the players in the circle sing and clap.
2. The señorita shakes parts of the body, or *every* part of the body. The other players imitate her.
3. The players wiggle and wobble and twist, slowly getting closer to the ground. Then they wiggle and wobble and twist higher and higher.
4. The señorita closes both eyes, sticks out a pointer finger, and turns around until everyone yells "Stop!" Whoever the señorita is pointing to at the end of the song must go into the middle of the circle and become the new "señorita."

1. I was go-ing to Ken-tuck-y, I was go-ing to the fair.
I met a señ-or-i-ta with flow-ers in her hair.

2. Oh, shake it, señ-or-i-ta, Shake and wave your hand.
Shake it like a milk-shake, a milk-shake in a can.

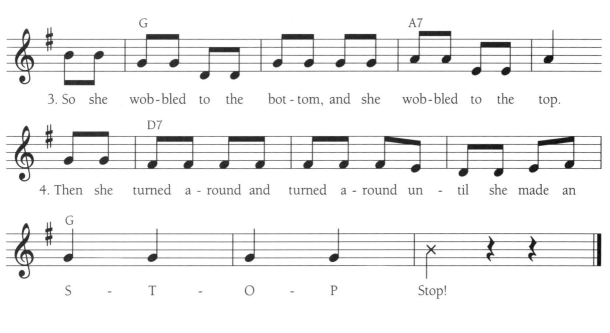

3. So she wob-bled to the bot-tom, and she wob-bled to the top.

4. Then she turned a-round and turned a-round un-til she made an

S - T - O - P Stop!

67

84 Green Grass Grows All Around

Play this as a challenge game: Each person takes a turn singing the final line of the song (the pile-up part). If you make a mistake or leave something our, *you're* out!

1. There was a tree (There was a tree) All in the wood (All in the wood),
2. Now, on that tree (Now, on that tree) There was a trunk (There was a trunk),

The pret-tiest lit-tle tree (The pret-tiest lit-tle tree)
The pret-tiest lit-tle trunk (The pret-tiest lit-tle trunk)

That you ev-er did see (That you ev-er did see).
That you ev-er did see (That you ev-er did see).

Verse 2 only
Oh, the tree in the wood,
Oh, the trunk on the tree and the tree in the wood, And the

Verse 1 *Chorus*

green grass grows all a-round, all a-round, And the green grass grows all a-round.

3. Now, on that trunk (Now, on that trunk)
   There was a limb (There was a limb).
   The prettiest little limb (The prettiest little limb)
   That you ever did see (That you ever did see).
   Oh, the limb on the trunk
      and the trunk on the tree
      and the tree in the wood

   Chorus

4. Now, on that limb (Now, on that limb)
   There was a branch (There was a branch).
   The prettiest little branch (The prettiest
      little branch)
   That you ever did see (That you ever did see).
   Oh, the branch on the limb
      and the limb on the trunk
      and the trunk on the tree
      and the tree in the wood

   Chorus

5. Now, on that branch (Now, on that branch)
   There was a nest (There was a nest).
   The prettiest little nest (The prettiest little nest)
   That you ever did see (That you ever did see).
   Oh, the nest on the branch
      and the branch on the limb
      and the limb on the trunk
      and the trunk on the tree
      and the tree in the wood

   Chorus

6. And in the nest (And in the nest)
   There was an egg (There was an egg).
   The prettiest little egg (The prettiest
      little egg)
   That you ever did see (That you ever did see).
   Oh, the egg in the nest
      and the nest on the branch
      and the branch on the limb
      and the limb on the trunk
      and the trunk on the tree
      and the tree in the wood

   Chorus

7. And in the egg (And in the egg)
   There was a bird (There was a bird).
   The prettiest little bird (The prettiest little bird)
   That you ever did see (That you ever did see).
   Oh, the bird in the egg
      and the egg in the nest
      and the nest on the branch
      and the branch on the limb
      and the limb on the trunk
      and the trunk on the tree
      and the tree in the wood

   Chorus

8. Now, on the bird (Now, on the bird)
   There was a feather (There was a feather).
   The prettiest little feather (The prettiest
      little feather)
   That you ever did see (That you ever did see).
   Oh, the feather on the bird
      and the bird in the egg
      and the egg in the nest
      and the nest on the branch
      and the branch on the limb
      and the limb on the trunk
      and the trunk on the tree
      and the tree in the wood

   Chorus

9. And from the feather (And from the feather)
   There was a bed (There was a bed).
   The prettiest little bed (The prettiest little bed)
   That you ever did see (That you ever did see).
   Oh, the bed from the feather
     and the feather on the bird
     and the bird in the egg
     and the egg in the nest
     and the nest on the branch
     and the branch on the limb
     and the limb on the trunk
     and the trunk on the tree
     and the tree in the wood

   Chorus

10. And on the bed (And on the bed)
    There was a child (There was a child).
    The prettiest little child (The prettiest
      little child)
    That you ever did see (That you ever did see).
    Oh, the child on the bed
      and the bed from the feather
      and the feather on the bird
      and the bird in the egg
      and the egg in the nest
      and the nest on the branch
      and the branch on the limb
      and the limb on the trunk
      and the trunk on the tree
      and the tree in the wood

    Chorus

▲ ▼ ▲

11. And then the child (And then the child)
    He planted a seed (He planted a seed).
    The prettiest little seed (The prettiest little seed)
    That you ever did see (That you ever did see).
    Oh, the seed from the child
      and the child on the bed
      and the bed from the feather
      and the feather on the bird
      and the bird in the egg
      and the egg in the nest
      and the nest on the branch
      and the branch on the limb
      and the limb on the trunk
      and the trunk on the tree
      and the tree in the wood

    Chorus

12. And from that seed (And from that seed)
    There grew a tree (There grew a tree).
    The prettiest little tree (The prettiest
      little tree)
    That you ever did see (That you ever did see).
    Oh, the tree from the seed
      and the seed from the child
      and the child on the bed
      and the bed from the feather
      and the feather on the bird
      and the bird in the egg
      and the egg in the nest
      and the nest on the branch
      and the branch on the limb
      and the limb on the trunk
      and the trunk on the tree
      and the tree in the wood

    Chorus

85 *Found a Peanut*

Do you know the melody of the song "Clementine"?
Then you don't *need* the music—
just sing these words to that tune!

1. Found a pea - nut, Found a pea - nut, Found a pea - nut right__ now.
Right__ now I found a pea - nut, Found a pea - nut right__ now.

2. It was rot - ten, It was rot - ten, It was rot - ten right__ now.
Right__ now it was__ rot - ten, It was rot - ten right__ now.

3. Ate it anyway,
   Ate it anyway,
   Ate it anyway right now.
   Right now I ate it anyway,
   Ate it anyway right now.

4. Got a stomachache,
   Got a stomachache,
   Got a stomachache right now.
   Right now I got a stomachache,
   Got a stomachache right now.

5. Called the doctor,
   Called the doctor,
   Called the doctor right now.
   Right now I called the doctor,
   Called the doctor right now.

6. Died anyway,
   Died anyway,
   Died anyway right now.
   Right now I died anyway,
   Died anyway right now.

   (Choke, gasp . . .)

86 A Hole in the Bucket

A boy (or boys) can sing the male part, and a girl (or girls) the female role; or a boy (or boys) can sing the female part in a high voice, while the girl (or girls) can perform the male role in deep, deep tones.

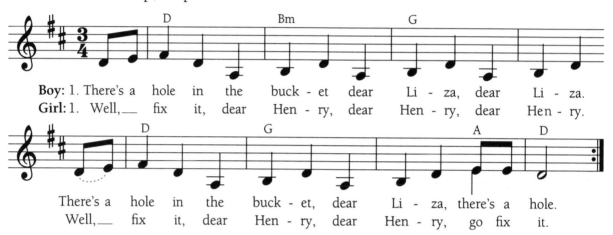

Boy: 1. There's a hole in the buck - et dear Li - za, dear Li - za.
Girl: 1. Well,— fix it, dear Hen - ry, dear Hen - ry, dear Hen - ry.

There's a hole in the buck - et, dear Li - za, there's a hole.
Well,— fix it, dear Hen - ry, dear Hen - ry, go fix it.

2. **Boy:** With what shall I fix it, dear Liza, dear Liza?
With what shall I fix it, dear Liza, with what?

   Girl: With a straw, dear Henry, dear Henry, dear Henry.
With a straw, dear Henry, dear Henry, with straw.

3. **Boy:** But the straw is too long, dear Liza, dear Liza.
But the straw is too long, dear Liza, too long.

   Girl: Then cut it, dear Henry, dear Henry, dear Henry.
Then cut it, dear Henry, dear Henry, then cut it.

4. **Boy:** Well, how shall I cut it dear Liza, dear Liza?
Well, how shall I cut it, dear Liza, well, how?

   Girl: With a knife, dear Henry, dear Henry, dear Henry.
With a knife, dear Henry, dear Henry, with a knife.

5. **Boy:** But the knife is too dull, dear Liza, dear Liza.
But the knife is too dull, dear Liza, too dull.

   Girl: Then sharpen it, dear Henry, dear Henry, dear Henry.
Then sharpen it, dear Henry, dear Henry, then sharpen it.

6. **Boy:** With what shall I sharpen it, dear Liza, dear Liza?
With what shall I sharpen it, dear Liza, with what?

   Girl: With a whetstone, dear Henry, dear Henry, dear Henry.
With a whetstone, dear Henry, dear Henry, with a whetstone.

7. **Boy:** But the whetstone's too dry, dear Liza, dear Liza.
   But the whetstone's too dry, dear Liza, too dry.

   Girl: Then wet it, dear Henry, dear Henry, dear Henry.
   Then wet it, dear Henry, dear Henry, then wet it.

8. **Boy:** With what shall I wet it dear Liza, dear Liza?
   With what shall I wet it, dear Liza, with what?

   Girl: With water, dear Henry, dear Henry, dear Henry.
   With water, dear Henry, dear Henry, with water.

9. **Boy:** Well, how shall I carry it, dear Liza, dear Liza?
   Well, how shall I carry it, dear Liza, well, how?

   Girl: In a bucket, dear Henry, dear Henry, dear Henry.
   In a bucket, dear Henry, dear Henry, in a bucket.

   Boy (*spoken impatiently*): But there's a hole in the bucket!

87 John Jacob Jingleheimer Schmidt

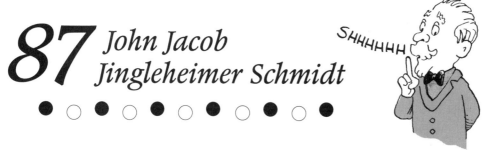

Each time you sing this song, get quieter and quieter . . . until you get to "There goes John Ja-cob Jin-gle-heim-er Schmidt, da-da-da-da-da-da-da," which is *shouted* each and every time, even when you are barely whispering the words of the first part of the song.

88 If You're Happy and You Know It

CLAP
CLAP

1. If you're hap-py and you know it, clap your hands. *(clap, clap)*

If you're hap-py and you know it, clap your hands. *(clap, clap)*

If you're hap-py and you know it, then your face will sure-ly show it.

If you're hap-py and you know it, clap your hands. *(clap, clap)*

2. . . . stamp your feet *(stamp, stamp)* . . .

3. . . . shout hooray ("Hooray!") . . .

4. . . . do all three *(clap, clap, stamp, stamp, "hooray!")* . . .

If you are accompanying yourself on the guitar, you can play this song in the key of E, using the chords A, E, and B7.

89 *John Brown's Baby*

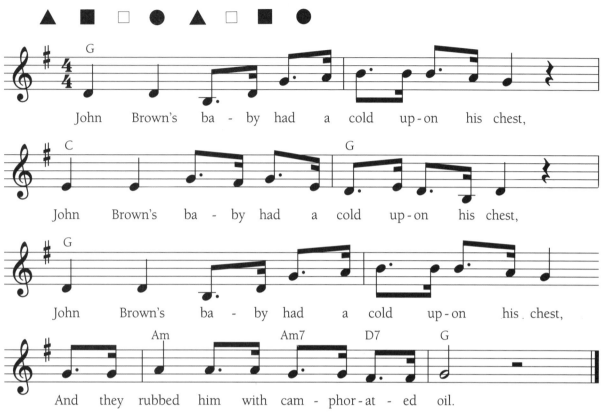

John   Brown's   ba - by   had   a   cold   up-on   his   chest,

John   Brown's   ba - by   had   a   cold   up-on   his   chest,

John   Brown's   ba - by   had   a   cold   up-on   his   chest,

And   they   rubbed   him   with   cam - phor-at - ed   oil.

Here are the motions that you do as you sing the words of this song:

John Brown's baby (*fold arms and rock the baby*) had a cold (*cough into your closed fist*) upon his chest (*slap chest*),

John Brown's baby (*fold arms and rock*) had a cold (*cough*) upon his chest (*slap chest*),

John Brown's baby (*fold arms and rock*) had a cold (*cough*) upon his chest (*slap chest*),

And they rubbed him (*rub chest*) with camphorated oil (*hold your nose—because camphorated oil has a bad smell*).

The first time sing the song through, then leave out the word "baby" (just do the motion). The next time, leave out the words "baby" and "cold" (etc.).

90 Let Everyone Join in the Game

Do the actions as you sing the words!

Let ev-ery-one clap hands with me, It's eas-y as eas-y can be.

Let ev-ery-one join in the game, *(clap clap)*,

You'll find that it's al-ways the same. *(clap clap)*.

Let ev-ery-one shake it with me, It's eas-y as eas-y can be.

Let ev-ery-one join in the game,

You'll find that it's al-ways the same.

Let ev-ery-one be ro-bots like me, It's eas-y as eas-y can be.

91 Little Bunny Foo-Foo

◇ ◆ ◇ ◆ ◇

Here's a song with a clever moral at the end, and here are the motions that go with it:

Sing 3 times

Lit-tle Bun-ny Foo Foo   hop-pin' through the for - est,

Scoop-in' up the field   mice,   and

bop-pin' 'em on the head.

(spoken)

Down came the Good Fairy, and she said, "Lit -tle Bun -ny Foo Foo,

I don't want to see you   scoop-in' up the field mice

and   bop-pin' 'em on the head.

1. I'll give you
2. I'll give you

two more chances, and if   you don't be - have, I'm gonna turn you
one more chance, and if   you don't be - have, I'm gonna turn you

into a goon."
into a goon."   The next   day:

Little Bunny

Scoopin'

Boppin'

Good Fairy

Chances

Goon

78

"I gave you three chances, and you didn't be - have. So now I'm gonna turn you into a goon." And poof, that's ex - actly what she did. And the moral of the story is: "Hare today, goon tomorrow!"

92 Michael Finnegan

Sing this song faster and faster as you go along. Then when you can't get any faster, slow it down as much as you can. If you sing it right, this song never ends!

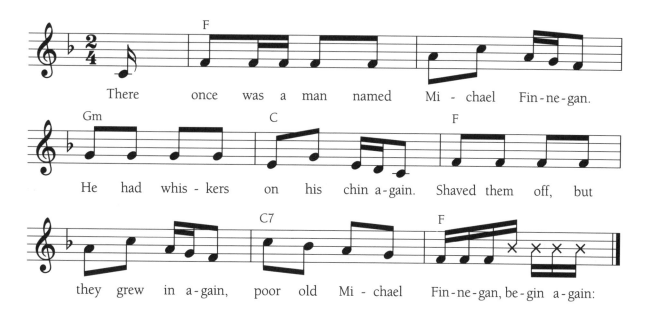

There once was a man named Mi - chael Fin - ne - gan. He had whis - kers on his chin a - gain. Shaved them off, but they grew in a - gain, poor old Mi - chael Fin - ne - gan, be - gin a - gain:

93 *Little Peter Rabbit*

▲ ▽ ▲ ▽ ▲ ▽ ▲ ▽ ▲

This song is sung to the melody of "John Brown's Baby."

Here are the motions:

On "little," show how little he is by holding out your pointer finger and thumb with a space in between.

On "rabbit," stick your pointer and your pinkie up like ears and hold your hand up to the back of your head.

On "fly," wave both arms at your sides.

On "hand," place your thumb and pointer finger together onto the palm of your other hand.

Repeat three times; on "he flicked it," flick your palm with your pointer and thumb.

On "it flew away," make a flapping motion at your sides with both arms.

Sing the song once, then start leaving out one more word and just doing the motion each time you repeat the song.

Lit – tle Pe – ter Rab – bit had a fly up-on his hand,

Lit – tle Pe – ter Rab – bit had a fly up-on his hand,

Lit – tle Pe – ter Rab – bit had a fly up-on his hand,

And he flicked it and it flew a – way.

94 Miss Mary Mack

△ □ ○ △ □ ○

This is a clapping song to be played with a friend.

On "Miss," slap your knees with both hands.

On "Mary," cross your arms and hit your opposite shoulders, then slap your knees again.

On "Mack," clap your hands together, then you're into the pattern of the song itself.

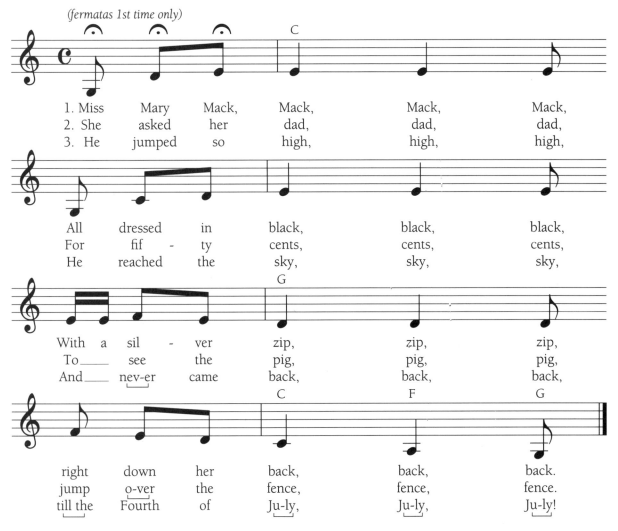

(fermatas 1st time only)

1. Miss Mary Mack, Mack, Mack, Mack,
2. She asked her dad, dad, dad,
3. He jumped so high, high, high,

All dressed in black, black, black,
For fif - ty cents, cents, cents,
He reached the sky, sky, sky,

With a sil - ver zip, zip, zip,
To_____ see the pig, pig, pig,
And_____ nev-er came back, back, back,

right down her back, back, back.
jump o-ver the fence, fence, fence.
till the Fourth of Ju-ly, Ju-ly, Ju-ly!

The pattern goes like this: *Clap, slap, clap, right, clap, left, clap, both.*

Clap (clap hands together)

Slap (slap hands on lap)

Right (clap your right hand against your partner's right hand)

Left (clap your left hand against your partner's left hand)

Both (clap both hands against your partner's two hands)

95 *Mushi Mushi*

This Japanese song is sung to the tune of "London Bridge."

As the Japanese kids sing it, they hold one hand up to their ears, as if that hand were a telephone, for this little ditty is a nonsensical telephone conversation.

Here are the words in Japanese. Pronounce 'em phonetically.

Mushi mushi
Ah-no-neh,
Ah-no-neh,
Ah-no-neh.
Mushi mushi
Ah-no-neh,
Ah-so des-ka.   (Hold the "*sooo*" part a bit longer, as you do when you sing "my *fair* lady.")

Here's what the words mean:

"Mushi mushi" means "Hello, hello."

"Ah-no-neh" has no real meaning. It's like "um," "er," or "well," with which we sometimes start a sentence when we're trying to think of what to say next.

"Ah-so deska" means "Is *that* so!"

Mu - shi mu - shi Ah - no neh,   Ah - no neh,   Ah - no neh,

Mu - shi mu - shi Ah - no neh,   Ah   so   des - ka.____

96 My Hat, It Has Three Corners

♦ ♦ ♦ ♦ ♦ ♦

The first time you sing this song, you can do motions with it:

On "my," point to yourself.
On "hat," touch your head.
On "three," hold up three fingers.
On "corners," point to your bent elbow (which is definitely a corner!).

When you have sung the song through once with all the motions, sing it four more times, each time leaving out one word and just "thinking" that word as you do the motion. (For example, on the second time through, you would not sing "my" when it came up in the song, but you would point to yourself. The third time through, you would not sing "my" or "hat," but you would point first to yourself and then to your head.) Continue until all four motions are acted out, but silent.

By the way, George Washington and his soldiers wore three-cornered hats, called tricornes. However, this is not an old American song; it comes from Germany.

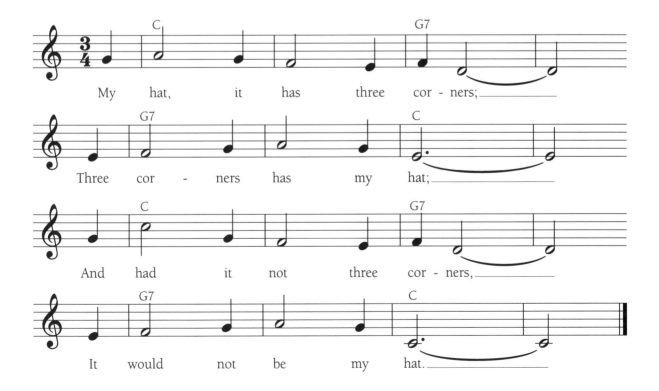

My hat, it has three cor - ners;
Three cor - ners has my hat;
And had it not three cor - ners,
It would not be my hat.

97 She'll Be Coming 'Round the Mountain

This Southern mountain song has phrases that are fun to shout at the end of each line. I'll bet you can figure out the motions that go with each of the phrases.

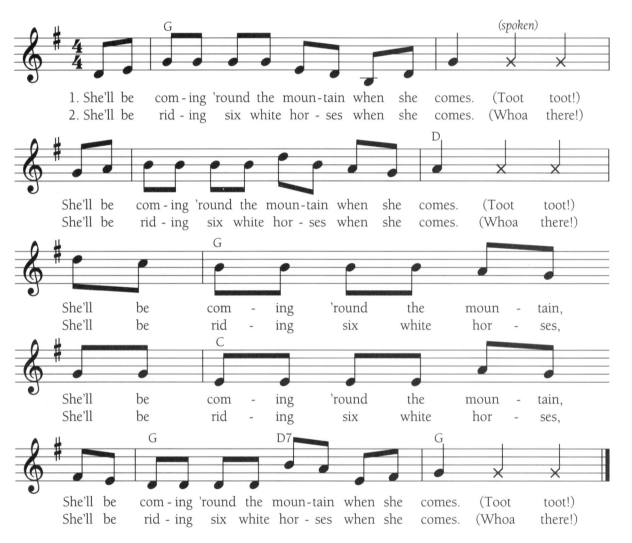

1. She'll be com-ing 'round the moun-tain when she comes. (Toot toot!)
2. She'll be rid-ing six white hor-ses when she comes. (Whoa there!)

She'll be com-ing 'round the moun-tain when she comes. (Toot toot!)
She'll be rid-ing six white hor-ses when she comes. (Whoa there!)

She'll be com - ing 'round the moun - tain,
She'll be rid - ing six white hor - ses,

She'll be com - ing 'round the moun - tain,
She'll be rid - ing six white hor - ses,

She'll be com-ing 'round the moun-tain when she comes. (Toot toot!)
She'll be rid-ing six white hor-ses when she comes. (Whoa there!)

3. Oh, we'll kill the old red rooster
   when she comes. (Chop, chop!)

4. Oh, we'll all have chicken and dumplings
   when she comes. (Yum, yum!)

5. Oh, we'll all go out to meet her
   when she comes. (Hi, there!)

98 Ten Green Bottles

Some people start this song with "ninety-nine bottles a-standing on the wall." You can start with any number you choose! The best part of this song is the fun of making the sound of the bottle crash at the end of the third line.

1. There are ten green bot-tles a-stand-ing on the wall.

There are ten green bot-tles a-stand-ing on the wall.

But if one green bot-tle should ac-ci-dent-'ly fall. (Crash!)

There'd be nine green bot-tles a-stand-ing on the wall.

2. There are nine green bottles a-standing on the wall.
There are nine green bottles a-standing on the wall.
But if one green bottle should accident'ly fall (Crash!),
There'd be eight green bottles a-standing on the wall.

Continue until there are no green bottles a-standing on the wall!

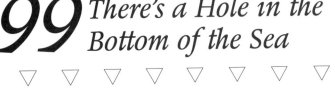

99 There's a Hole in the Bottom of the Sea

1. There's a hole in the bot-tom of the sea.____
2. There's a { log in the / hole in the } bot-tom of the sea.____

There's a hole in the bot-tom of the sea.____
There's a { log in the / hole in the } bot-tom of the sea.____

There's a hole,____ There's a hole,____
There's a log,____ There's a log,____

There's a hole in the bot-tom of the sea.____
There's a { log in the / hole in the } bot-tom of the sea.____

3. There's a bump on the log in the hole in the bottom of the sea.
   There's a bump on the log in the hole in the bottom of the sea.
   There's a bump, There's a bump,
   There's a bump on the log in the hole in the bottom of the sea.

4. There's a frog on the bump on the log in the hole in the bottom of the sea.
   There's a frog on the bump on the log in the hole in the bottom of the sea.
   There's a frog, There's a frog,
   There's a frog on the bump on the log in the hole in the bottom of the sea.

5. There's a fly on the frog on the bump on the log in the hole in the bottom of the sea.
    There's a fly on the frog on the bump on the log in the hole in the bottom of the sea.
    There's a fly, There's a fly,
    There's a fly on the frog on the bump on the log in the hole in the bottom of the sea.

6. There's a wing on the fly on the frog on the bump on the log in the hole in the bottom of the sea.
    There's a wing on the fly on the frog on the bump on the log in the hole in the bottom of the sea.
    There's a wing, There's a wing,
    There's a wing on the fly on the frog on the bump on the log in the hole in the bottom of the sea.

7. There's a flea on the wing on the fly on the frog on the bump on the log in the hole in the bottom of the sea.
    There's a flea on the wing on the fly on the frog on the bump on the log in the hole in the bottom of the sea.
    There's a flea, There's a flea,
    There's a flea on the wing on the fly on the frog on the bump on the log in the hole in the bottom of the sea.

100 Three Jolly Fishermen

1. There were three jol - ly fish - er - men,
2. The first one's name was A - bra - ham,

There were three jol - ly fish - er - men,
The first one's name was A - bra - ham,

Fish - er, fish - er, men - men - men, Fish - er, fish - er, men - men - men,
A - bra, A - bra, ham - ham - ham, A - bra, A - bra, ham - ham - ham,

There were three jol - ly fish - er - men.
The first one's name was A - bra - ham.

3. The second one's name was Isaac,
   The second one's name was Isaac,
   I, I, zak-zak-zak,
   I, I, zak-zak-zak,
   The second one's name was Isaac.

4. The third one's name was Jacob,
   The third one's name was Jacob,
   Ja, Ja, cub-cub-cub,
   Ja, Ja, cub-cub-cub,
   The third one's name was Jacob.

5. They all sailed up to Jericho,
   They all sailed up to Jericho,
   Jerry, Jerry, co-co-co,
   Jerry, Jerry, co-co-co,
   They all sailed up to Jericho.

6. They wished they'd gone to Amsterdam,
   They wished they'd gone to Amsterdam,
   Amster, Amster, sh-sh-sh,
   Amster, Amster, sh-sh-sh,
   They wished they'd gone to Amsterdam.

7. You shouldn't have said that naughty word,
   You shouldn't have said that naughty word,
   Naughty, naughty, word-word-word,
   Naughty, naughty, word-word-word,
   You shouldn't have said that naughty word!

101 *This Old Man*

The motions that I have always done to the words of this song are:

Clap your hands together.

Slap your lap.

Clap you hands together.

Clap left hands with your partner.

Clap your hands together.

Clap right hands with your partner.

(Repeat)

Repeat the pattern until you get to the line "give your dog a bone." On "give your dog a," roll your hands over and under each, moving them *away* from you. On "bone," extend your palms (so that everybody can see the bone). On "this old man came rolling home," roll your hands back *toward* yourself.

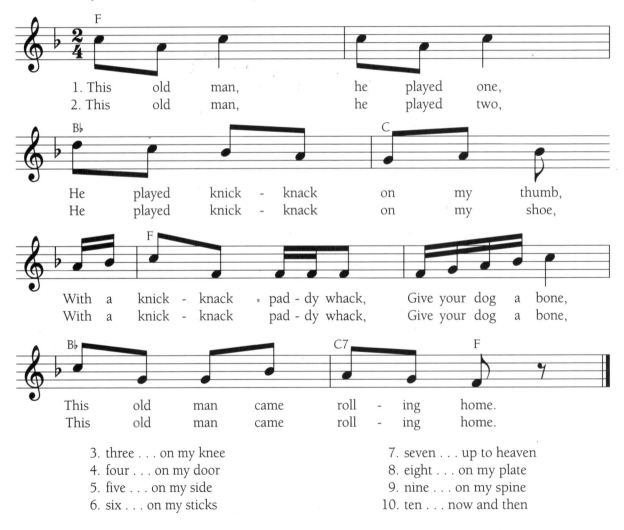

1. This old man, he played one,
2. This old man, he played two,

He played knick - knack on my thumb,
He played knick - knack on my shoe,

With a knick - knack pad - dy whack, Give your dog a bone,
With a knick - knack pad - dy whack, Give your dog a bone,

This old man came roll - ing home.
This old man came roll - ing home.

3. three . . . on my knee
4. four . . . on my door
5. five . . . on my side
6. six . . . on my sticks

7. seven . . . up to heaven
8. eight . . . on my plate
9. nine . . . on my spine
10. ten . . . now and then